"Dishonor before
death"

John Woods
1963
Kalamazoo

ON THE MORNING OF COLOR

no. 22 *in*

Indiana University Poetry Series

BY JOHN WOODS

On the Morning of Color

INDIANA UNIVERSITY PRESS

BLOOMINGTON   1 9 6 1

for C. W. *and* D. W., *with sufficient reason*

FOR PERMISSION to reprint certain of the poems in this book, acknowledgments are due to the editors of *Poetry*, *The Paris Review*, *Fresco*, *Calliope*, *The Saturday Review*, *Prairie Schooner*, *The Massachusetts Review*, and *Poetry Northwest*.

CONTENTS

part 1

WHEN SENSES FLED

I am custodian of close things.
Even winter trees have blurred
To leaf, and faces come upon me
Suddenly. I am a startled man
To half the town, and half my yard
Is blunderland. First, I lost
The violets, then the grass,
And now, the red and wren white fence.
Farewell, the bright decay of oak,
The crewcut water, the black assizes
Of the night. Farewell, the visual.

Today, the wind began to lag
And all its freight of season drained
Into the neighbor trees. And all
The smoking, sideburned streets
Dropped ashes on the muted playground.
Let lightning slam the screen, I cry,
Let neighbors war, a shop of cats
Tear metal. O stone me with shouting.
But the grating thunderhead suspends
Its buzzing nest beneath my bough.
Farewell, the audible.

                    Touch,
Tell me what the world displays
For now I rain behind my eyes.
If you would hurt me, gather close,
For in the last deception, skin,
I must be broken by a kiss.
Love is a cave of scrolls, and I
Have thrown away all spectacles.
I roll horizons like a hoop
Among the mufflered trees, and see
Nerve ends crackling in the dark.
Farewell, the tangible.

                    Inside,
I stand, a coalescent dust.
When I sing, my voices turn
To stone, and where I touch, veins
Stand out. When I am alone, the forest
Swarms with nakedness, and where
I point, pole stars waltz along
My finger. Look, the fence appears,
Then grass. And all my senses step
On naked feet into the garden
To ring, an anvil of the storm,
To name the kneeling animals.

POEM AT THIRTY

for David

On the morning of noise
Our eyes kindled the hills.
Wind put the smallest leaves to our love.
With walnut hands we wrung the great coiled flight
From bitterns and other long birds
Of the long morning.
Windtips blurred on the cedar
In persuasions of tilt and glide, give way
And spring back, touch wood and run home.

If we cried cold, the streams rang like bells
Through tiers of oaks,
And a brown sun circled the horizon;
And weeping, trailing mufflers of coarse flame,
We chopped for fish and bombed the shelterhouse
With disappearing snow.
If we cried stop,
Bright occasions held their slide
From flaming oak to shale alley.
On tip and toe the fishing birds
Would weld upon their diving images.

On the morning of color,
On the morning of first-seen,
When every acorn rolled into place,
When every child seemed the final incident of poise,
When the great waters
Were one small stream carrying out to river
The reflective world,

We could not sing of love or loss,
Or count to thirty, holding our breath.

But now we say, God, sun,
Circumstance, whatever riddles us,
Send us one such morning to grow on.

Driven to his garden, his woodworking tools,
From the blaze of his own work, making his study
Uninhabitable, he pulled terrible anchors.
Always, in the rout beyond his hedge
Where even dust had lost its innocence,
Were those who'd write down everything he said
And sell it back to him as news, as truth.
What could he command outside the fence?
All the lovely causes. Once outside
His gate, he found a golden podium.
Once, when steel went up, he found a sign:
Love thy neighbor as he loves himself.
Outside his lawn, he thought, were many truths.

But after mitres, varnish and rottonstone,
After pruning, peatmoss and a cross of roses,
After Israel, after mail, and after dinner
Where he fed on his own crisp lettuce hearts,
There was the burning corridor, the smoking door,
The desk, flaring with his own great vision,
Which he must seize and strike with bare fire,
Or down with tears for the ordinary world.

PLAYWRIGHT

1

(Suspecting hollow trees, the barn to be
Held together by the manes of hay,)
The pickshank surrey with its sail of webs,
I poked around the yard, kicking weeds.
Manure reassured me, the voiding mare,
And rain that swept the picnic under elms,
That more than painted canvas stood around.

I cast my images to every wind.
Milkweed, plantain, chickweed, mustard, buckhorn
Burst again from notched and drying furrows,
Again in wagon track, and once more swarmed
In wild and wooly sheep pen, boiling seeds
And bees into the air. *Order,* I cried,
Order, sitting by the dry stream bed,
And start again.
                 Wondering if the trees
Were full of air, the barn was swept together
By brooms of hay, or held by atmospheric
Pressure to the surrey with its vacuum horse
A-prance . . .
             Order, winked the dry stream stones.
The world is reaffirmed by sweet compost.

Think in acts, the preacher and the teacher
Said; in scenes, my mother and another
Warned; in symbols, ironies and myth
Said all the seedless, seedy Criticals.
Which is the play? Look at the world until
It thins: the overthrust of meeting oaks
Refines into proscenium, the arcs

Of swallows are the moths of summer stock,
The backlog in the willow close becomes
The greenroom with an arty couch; and, crouched,
The hunter and his dog with nose alight
Become the critics from the New York *Times*.

Again: oppressed by paper trees, afraid
The barn was a cleverness of brushwork,
In short, afraid of art, I pinched myself.
The stream sprang back, the sparrows bobbed for apples,
The play lay neatly stacked beside my bed.

2

Look at the water. It tells the sky.
Look at the sky. It tells the way
That all the casuals of eye
Can richen to a voice, and say:
Shiftiness is absolute,
So be a prince of enterprise.
The banner falters from its root.
A little breeze destroys the skies.

Or so I wrote at twenty-five.
A lovely concept, honestly
Arrived at through experience.
If change is all, let every sense
Ring jubilance and gramercy!
Wide to the world and broad alive!

But this destroyed my poetry.
When Frost denied his glacial fence
He failed to see the strongest gyve
Is verse of place. One must connive
With rebel leaders in their tents.
Only at home must one be free.

The play is not the thing, but dense
Enough with life for Lear to shrive
Us with a family, the angry
Genes of Adam's curse; to die
With every surrogate, to wive
Our mothers, kill our innocence.

The villain, ingenue, and clown
Crackle at my finger tips.
The cave of night, the praising town
Swing in my orbit, and at your lips
You make a god of cold precision;
And heaven, a critic's indecision.
I cast my selves into the day.
Your faces flicker, well and ill.
I walk apart; and parallel,
You almost risk my life in play,
Until the final curtains spill.
Then, safe until the matinee.

LIGHTING TECHNICIAN

In the beginning, there was dimness,

>What light fell
>On Morning One?

Except the exits, promising for some

>The waters roll
>Above and down.

A way out: Mars with blood in his eye,

>What set flew
>And which stayed down?

Brothels, high radio reefs for swimming planes.

>Turn on the blue,
>Switch on the lawn,

Then, the single spot. The sun hangs on the cyclorama.

>Roll on a tree,
>Slide on its double.

Things rise to the surface of the eye: five chairs,

>They mingle seed.
>And all our trouble

A table, tape recorder, dixie cup, look away, look away.

>Begins when suns
>Commence to tick

When the light drew back, the eye stepped forth

    And wind us in
    The dying clock.

Into darkness. Everything since, an afterimage.

    On Morning Five,
    Hardly a whale

Tinge the Lovescene red, the Recognition blue.

    Is not alive.
    O Duplicate!

Fade out the Farewell at the Station, flick neon

    O Mimeograph!
    Male and Female

On the Strangers at the Hotel, heighten

    (Wait for the laugh)
    Are cued onstage.

Miss DeMur with yellow when she enters the Garden,

    Though Playwright's heaven
    Is the actor's curse,

In the beginning.

    On Morning Seven,
    We rehearse.

THE FLOOD

First the sandbar dipped; then winter's
Thatch of twigs fell down. It was night
All week upriver; rain and its hints
Darkened dirt until it ran.
Brown foam bloomed around the snags.
What came up in Billy's barn?
A raft of corncobs and a slickered rat.
What lay down in Billy's field?
A big brown udder of a river.

Mr. Arnold's wheat went under next.
Yesterday, a shoot of water entered,
Hogging the corncrib, taking all room.
Now the river wrinkles in the porchswing,
Driftwood clusters at the garden gate,
And the woodpile rises off somewhere.
All the light and loose, yea, has risen.

The map is plunging under, the bridge is down,
The operator holds a conch of seas.
And on the rooftops of the sinking world,
We turn from one another, for love and all
Its selfish groupings close us in ourselves:
The nail of sex we drove into our thigh;
Home, that didn't fail us soon enough;
And pride, on which we squatted, grunting images.
But now we look inside, and in the flood
We see the glowing freeways of the mind.

THE DEAF MAN

That splintered day, that week of railing winds
And hard water, that month of eiderdown,
His world drew back, past the hanging barn
He read stars through, further than the lake
With its bleach of sand, the waters ironing the grass,
Until he heard nothing but his booming head.
The wind read his lips, and he saw such singing
As there was, shocked before him like the winter wheat.

Wet, stacked landscapes steamed in the morning
When only the sky rang blue. Behind his head
The birds thundered, the wormy oaks sang madrigals.
Now his wife shrilled to her ears the spars of clutter
And second choices, and her anchor sparked
On the stony hills and armored corn.

But he grew around her in such a poise
He seemed a millglass sterned around a reed.
As snow floured the panblack hills, love returned,
A channel swimmer in a spray of silence, where
In snow geese evenings they floated
In the featherbed. Then, urged beside her
In an Australian crawl, he sang of love Down Under.

The world is burning. Rust
Flickers in the harrow.
The long-dividing dust
Simmers in the marrow.
And girls will dazzle by
With flame at breast and thigh.

A porchswing rides the flood.
The mind goes under thrice
In the millrace of the blood,
Or thickens into ice.
Whatever men devise
The corporeal denies.

The wind that blows my tongue
Until I think I sing,
In every tree has sung,
And will sing, everything.
The wind blows through my bones.
Which is the one that moans?

The gods that blessed the earth
Have long been out of town.
Though dirt invented birth,
The signposts still point down.
This mustering of grief
Still totters with the leaf.

THE WAY OUT

I say this step is first:
Shake your father's hand
But let it fall away
To wallet or to wand.
Unless you would be cursed
Walk outward from his shape
And the memory of rape.

The next step is the worst.
Untie your mother's arms
And let them reach unfed;
Don't hear her soft alarms.
Though every man has nursed,
You'll take a narrow bed
And a narrow plate for bread.

And when you break your staff
And drown your book for love,
Draw back the inner eye,
Watch strangers from above.
Or you'll hear your father laugh,
And beneath you, where you lie,
You'll hear your mother sigh.

TO THE WAITERS FOR MIRACLES

You will not gather pears again in blue aprons,
Nor poach the buff deer.
There are no kings worth dying for.
Nor will you see the black loam turned,
The wind come back, and wheel again
In its green springing.

No luck will save you, nor faith
In a letterhead. No benefactor shall name you heir.
For names shall die, and no horseman
Suddenly visible, nor non-stop serum,
Nor bread from stone
Shall stop the fall of stone.

No woman again, no, not ever,
Her hour come upon her, shall lie in the beak
Of God, deaf in the artillery
Of wings, and make of her own blood and milk
A thin bearer of flesh for more or less
Than our skin's sake.

Nor you, singer, worn by song
To the quick of your throat, nor you,
Poet, riding the undulant wave of language
Near coasts where man in the shot dark
Fights your ancient war in chaos
And animal cries . . .

THE NOSTOPATH

I thought no other place
Could sing so many birds,
Surpass with hill and tree
My mustering of words,
Where deeper than I see,
The streams reflect my face.

But doesn't every stream
Reflect a common day
To James or Baudelaire;
And nightly entropy
Turn here to anywhere
When the passport is a dream?

The fountain's open shock,
The waveform in the pond,
The spiral at the drain,
Though true in any land,
This truth is in the vein,
The vein runs through the rock.

Wind will filter through
The barbed wire at the pass;
The soldiers at the door
Will have the wrong address;
Their swords will melt before
The acids of the dew.

NEAR CARTER'S MILL

By walked-along water, the trees hang fire.
The roundhouse wind gives blood to my cheek.
In loved-down grass, by nesting air,
The hare lies gathered, tight and quick.
And near the shalebed, rundown stream,
The millwheel stands in the spraying flume.

From whistle-far town beyond the wheel
Where a Sunday sky, ringing with clouds,
Holds dusty horizons of October hills,
I fled this morning the well-drawn words
Of the preacher with his turning tongue
To the trembling wheel where racewaters lunge.

Under the quiet millstone reels
The browbeaten hill in an autumn rain,
The scored gulleys floundering downhill,
The bent-tined lightning, and the veins
Of thunder cracking the roiling ore.
The millstone trembles on the leafdrift floor.

When walked-alone water, by the falling trees,
Says, This is your book with a windy page,
Where the wet thumb counts and the wet eye grieves,
Then the deep heart thunders against the age.
By overboard water, I strike as stone.
I blow the grist and seize the grain.

O faraway town with your prince and poor,
I stand six miles up Lincoln Road
Where time held close, while the world went over
To the elbowing town where wheels go mad,
Where the factories spew by the granary,
With bread for you, but none for me.

Told, then told again, by night,
In rain blurring the fathom lights
And smoothing the palm-and-knuckled bay.
Told by night when eyelids shape
A microverse of flares, pinwheels and shooting dust.
Told by the crossed trees and the river,
Changing its place with rain, and the salts
Of seven white-rimmed and fishful seas.
Told by the scrabbling poor in the wet shards of the city,
By lands-end, precipice, parapet and afterlife, told:

Pray to bread, that it still rise,
Waxed against the vein of dissolution.
Pray to culture, that bread may live beyond its day of yeast.
Pray to money, that it sweeten the miser in his last vault.
(And how, in its dispensation, like the early death of leaves.)
Pray to animals, O Ignorant, for they may judge us yet.
Pray to all the gods, for they are what we mean by images.
To wind, for it moves the woodsmoke across the willow-
    brake.
To rain, for the burning web of streetlights in the black tree.
To dung, for it completes the cadence which began with
    seed.
And pray to fire for what we learn in ashes.
And I was told this in the pelting season,
In dry grass, by all the torn, shed, waved, and pawned
Attributes of the solid world. Nothing I was born with
Is worth throwing away.

POEM BY WATER

Well met beside the attitudes of water,
We spent the day beneath the creaking bridge
That led from cornland into factories.
Beneath our hanging images the fish
Were poised between the reeds and smoking slag;
Above our shadows, the green and scorching wind.

Our words of love were shaken in the wind
That broke a wheel of ridges in the water.
Although we called on fire, the belching slag
Built its burial mounds beneath the bridge
And, upside down, betrayed the sliding fish
Who hoped for parks but entered factories.

We know the fields of corn are factories.
Like smoke, their tassels tower in the wind.
They spread their lungs beneath the earth as fish
Beneath the creek, and weave the sun and water
Into grain. Two worlds are one beneath the bridge;
A single sunlight greens the cooling slag.

And when the fire has frozen in the slag,
The glazing residues are factories
Of color, glacial masonry, a bridge
Of stone through which the colors wind.
But poisons fatten in the oily water,
The surface thickening with floating fish.

But we lie down as lovers, not as fish.
We see the steam that rises from the slag;
It is our breath, our heritage of water.
But words of love are lost in factories
Where all is knotted, knotted as the wind
That tilts the rasping weeds beneath the bridge.

The corn is loud. It tells another bridge
That links us, one to one; that links the fish
To spawning when rocks lay melting in the wind,
When men had fins and mountains leaped from slag.
I say these worlds are one: the factories
Discharging smoke, the corn distilling water;

I say we walk a bridge as old as wind.
O let us enter factories of water,
Breathe love on slag, and turn it into fish.

MAINE SCENE

Thin in the milkweed,
Wet by the fishery,
Tall by the linden,
The wind and the windcock
Turn on the season.

Robins had warned me
Music can tighten,
Thinner and harder,
Like wind in the basswood
Sung below hearing.

What is the reason?
White in the bindweed.
What is the reason?
Brown in the fairway.
What is the reason?

The axe in the heartwood
Two ridges over
Is seen before hearing,
Heard before falling
And falls out of living.

That is the reason
The true song is native,
Stays out the winter.
The pond ice will loosen
And kingfishers come.

That is the reason.
The fire in the hearth
Is the birth of the tree.
Love will come singing
From the hearth of the heart.

part 2

SUBURBAN NOTE

Give me an old practitioner
Who wears a dark device
To turn my middle inside out
And run my marrows ice.

We love our women by the book
With twenty-three positions:
1) Put it there, 2) Wind it up,
3) See Table Nine for visions.

Send me a wild adventuress
Who forgets to wind the clock,
Who locks me in an iron safe
Then tampers with the lock.

Send me that sweet inventoress
Who forgets to wrap the bread,
Who rings the changes with her toes
Upon the brass bedstead,

Who forgets to set the thermostat,
And wears a feather boa,
Who rides the chaste and glacial sheets,
A rumbling Krakatoa.

Now, Noah said, "These are the rules
You creatures must obey:
Keep your hatches firmly closed,
No smoking in the hay."

"Elephants, restrain yourselves,
We've room for only two.
Such exercise would spring our strakes
And dunk us in the blue."

"The latrine detail will form a line.
Whoever designed this raft
Forgot that we would soon go down
If all went pushing aft."

"No dice, no dancing, no unions, please.
Take care with whom you dine.
The brotherhood of animals
Is only party line."

So Noah lectured to the beasts
Until his voice grew thin;
Man before the Innocents,
Telling how to sin.

He felt the furnace of their breath;
Their eyes were burning near.
Then the tiger raised his paw
And sprang his sabers clear:

"Man, we are custodians
Of all the sparks of life.
Now take your notes and podium
And lecture to your wife."

"Your whale oil lamps have guttered
In the temples of your pride,
And no one wears my gaudy coat
Above the midnight tide."

Noah threw his sounding line
But pulled up wet laundry.
"We are the last of life," he cried,
"Above the groaning sea."

"We are the last alive," he prayed,
"Beneath the bursting sky."
"You are the last that live," he heard,
"In all the galaxy."

And so he climbed the creaking mast
To where the yardarm crossed;
And Noah, in his high lookout,
Played solitaire, and lost.

THE DEPARTMENTAL

a foxtrot

Once I lived on Barley Row,
  Fed roses from my hand,
Now I watch semesters grow,
    Sing 'postrophe, sing comma and.
      O gradebook, bluebook, textbook O
      How does your tenure grow?

I reviewed a book called *Sudden Bed*
  By Tilly Almsdale Rubbish.
The department head rose from the dead,
    Singing publish, publish, publish.
      O hexbook, blacklist, footnote O
      Where'd that Fellowship go?

Wabash threw old Ezra out,
  State U. sent Dylan packing.
Shakespeare couldn't teach Joe Lout
    With his N.E.A. card lacking.
      O loyalty, loyalty, loyalty Oath
      How's your Faculty Growth?

The ladies pour, the scholars bore,
  The janitor has the key.
The teaching fellows bow before
    The Terminal Degree.
      O doubleday, backbite, office space O
      How does your lecture know?

THE DRY EDGE

Look in, through the dry hedge;
The garden is leaves and a shuffle of crows.
The sundial, near the bramble edge,
Is telling the day, and the day slows.

Down on her knees, my potted aunt
Is rubbing some color into a rose.
No one tells her that you can't.
There is no calendar she knows.

Her old voice cracks in the freezing hush.
The winter gathers, the winter blows.
Round and round the mulberry bush
She shall have summer wherever she goes.

RUNNING A TEMPERATURE

Straight down, the noon was boarding up the trees.
Only shadows moved, toadstool squat
Beneath the driveway stone. The gaities
Of birdland closed. The heat was on our spot.

In every livingroom, the years of wax,
Of soap and frying seized us by the breath.
We sat in candlemolds, in buckwheat stacks,
And watched the green lawnsnake curl up in death.

UNCOMMITTED WEATHER

Uncommitted weather
Pauses near the gate.
Each would let the other
Dominate the day.
So narrowly they cleave
That neither one can leave.

Half of autumn hangs
And half has flared to earth.
Ice and water hinge
And neither swings in first.
How long can they embrace
In this disputed place?

Because I could not choose
I slept a warring night.
Uneasily I knew
The wind was blowing straight.
The morning light revealed
Decision held the field.

SONG FOR COLD COUNTRY

At the end of every lane
The shutters of the rain
Lock the pasture down.
Brown blasts the green.

The cistern breaks the pail,
A mirror slows the mill,
I carry coal and pour
Midnight on the fire.

The tower of the wind
Sinks into the sand
With the princess still asleep
In manacles of sleet.

THE BEACH

Waves dig in along the shore.
Gulls are luffing up the land.
Silent as a blade of ore,
A virgin glitters in the sand.

The sun bears down on breasts and thighs,
On lips that blur with ambergris,
On men with running tarts for eyes,
Whose tongues are burning in the breeze.

Each momentary lover stares,
A barefaced boy on burning decks.
The fallout from her Bikini tears
A path down every Middlesex.

THE RAKE

The nurse behind her apron
Was twisted into tears.
Mother threw her hands up
And called the Grenadiers.
The Colonel cried, "You blaggart!"
And towed me by the ears.
Sang the Rake, the Rake,
The nasty Rake.

I violated Alice
In the Morgan County Seat.
Her mother thought me dreadful
But later said, "My sweet."
And when the Parson caught us
He too was indiscreet
With the Rake, the Rake,
The ambiguous Rake.

I meddled with the goldfish
And herons in the lake,
Buttercups and daisies
And even chocolate cake!
So do not blame the yeast
When biscuits start to quake
With the Rake, the Rake,
The salty Rake.

IMAGINE ALL OUR POETS SINGING

Imagine all our poets singing, cheek
To jowl, their great beards blowing out,
Their boots, though none too clean, astamp
On some vast stage with strippers in the wings.
Shakespeare's at the Wurlitzer. He plays
By ear, of course, too loudly and too well.

The Lakers do a Lockestep, but Wordsworth
Trips, and falls upon his Boehme. (This pun
By courtesy of Byron, the lord whose life
Was scored for organ.) Blake, in tyger skin,
Goes flying with the scenery. Though Auden
Follows close, his motor conks from lack
Of fuel; he glides to rest at some girls' school.

Now Roethke, with his motley on, goes buck-
And-wing and pretty-prance with Yeats,
While Freud and A. E. Housman play the bongos.

The houselights dim, the clericals drift forward:
Donne and Herbert, Swift and Eliot,
Emerson and Byron in disguise.
O piety! O sanctitude! O God!
The wings are echoing their cloven dance.

A few retire, Winters, Tate, and Blackmur
Lead a group across the street, to where
The M. L. A. has just discovered Thomas
Was a Platonist (through Victor Hugo).

A few, whose sanity or passports weren't
In order, crowd in late: Kit Smart, the Pound,
John Clare and Edgar Guest, that radical
(The M. L. A. unmasked him through his meters).

Pulling weights and shifting scenes, assisting
With the makeup, the stand-ins hum their parts.
Engle's angels flap their shortcropped wings.
Santayana, Oscar Williams, Ellen
Bordon Stevenson, Ciardi, Hillyer.
(The guest list was prepared by Untermeyer.)

Outside, the marquee blares: A Thousand Poets
(Count them) On Our Mighty Stage! In smaller
Letters: See Emily half-rhyme! See Shelley,
Hart Crane, Sidney Keyes, and Masters
Do the high dive! See Eliot at prayer!

Imagine all our poets singing, verse
On verse, the cracked, the wheezed, the truly sung,
In some vast Amphitheatre, with Shakespeare
At the Wurlitzer.
                    Imagine also
Some applause. There is no audience.

ACCLAMATION

All that April, groundrack
hailed the orchard, and in
the rootcoil of lightning boiled
white clouds of dogwood.
All that April it was rain
straight down. Winter bellowed
far back in the ear.
Sun burst from ice
and the peeled stick of wind
pitched in slant elms,
and humping in the stands
of green, the thrown back
earth was alive with curling
toes of seeds.
          All April
in one night, when the ceiling
ran with clouds, and the stars,
for once in their lights, sang,
and walls fell in the perched
and booming branch until
the bridge shook, the air
struck between its coming
and growing. Then all
the nightlights out save where
the furrows burned blue,
the violets arced in deep
sheathes, and the coming
rose breathed red.
All the ice of the black
stream ran in sheets with eyes
cut out for holes, all night.

All that first daylight,
The green gray peeling
of the earth curved back,
And Robin Red, the loose
unready ladies of the unlatched
cottages, and all the shag-
tailed gods came dancing forth.

when?

part 3

LIE CLOSED, MY LATELY LOVED

Lie closed, my lately loved, in the far bed
At the foot of the moon, barred by sash and shade.
Now your eyes are shells adrift in shadow,
The fires banked. Under the furled sheets,
The long sloop of your body swings about
The anchor of a dream. The dark applause
Of leaves wakes in the wind the ear makes
When it hears no wind; the sapling bows
Against the wall in the footlight of the moon.

One hour away from sweating animals,
Afraid to wake the children or themselves,
We're locked apart, though something of your shape
Still molds my hand. I breathe you still.
I breathe the gross, the delicate, together.
I build a vision from our mingled dreams.
A heavy stallion rumbles in the straw,
The stud for all the trembling mares. Around
His yellow mouth hang crumbs of flowers.

IN MY DARKEST AGE

In my darkest age
I loved your medieval
Lips that dripped with gall
And honey in their rage.
I hung upon their feast
And gorged like any beast.

In a duel of tongues
Your kisses let out blood.
Beneath your falcon's hood
I urged such tender songs
That, gentled by such pap,
You fed me from your lap.

But last night in your cell
I heard the shadows speak
That others, drawn and weak,
Had swung within your bell
And made the armor boom
Across the freezing room.

I lie this lonely hour
And hold you, ignorance.
I know what renaissance
Is knocking at the tower.
But when the towers spill,
I'll swing, your clapper still.

1

Down among the rains, my dear,
I hear your pleasure lies.
Lord Brand will send his soldiers there;
Your lover soon will die.

I know you hid a blade, lady,
To give his throat a grin.
But lock your favors, thigh to thigh,
And cut him from within.

Who is your faithful counselor
Who gives such cruel advice?
Lord Kane, a bolt upon his door,
His lady carved of ice.

Where is the fox?
Where is the hound?
Both turned the corner
Under the ground.

Where is the hunter
With his black gun?
Fallen to earth
And beside him his son.

Where is the wife
That no one possessed?
Alive, with the fox
Red at her breast.

THE FAREWELL

Farewell the plum,
The underbelly,
Grape and bum
And eyeball jelly.
    Farewell the lung
    And veinous tongue.

Farewell the lush
And moistened hips,
Adenoidal gush
Of steaming lips.
    Farewell the globe
    And throbbing lobe.

Then leached to bone
Let poems rise,
Torn from stone
For stony eyes,
    Blind and bright
    With empty light.

AGAIN THE QUIET NIGHT

Again the quiet night,
And the alderbush is quick with birds,
Those treble insights
With their furnaced hearts.

Again the land,
And the vegetal beast called countryside
Is poised on stem and tendril
Above the rocking soil.

Again the green
Is black, but pressing green
On closed shades, on moth-drumming screens
Of simmering cabins.

Again the hands of the lovers
Brim with sweetness where they are closed
In the black of the green
Of the night.

The hill is born in fire
Again, and the windthrown
Birds thicken the trees
Until the trees are singing
And the hill is worn by fire.

Again the dogs are hunting
In the wet bark of the wood;
Treetops break into smoke
As the windfed birds are tossed
From the dogs and hunting fire.

The hill hides under wings
Where the night-jarred birds sing
Until the hill is singing,
And a dog hunts his lost bark
In the wet hide of the hill.

O we sang, two in the bush,
That a bird in the hand
Of the four-tined wind flew
Beneath our forking hide
On the firetorn hill again.

SESTINA

When my lady sings, the pitch is true,
The bird she masters whistles in her throat.
She captures music, and yet her captives move.
The swart guitarist leans against the wall,
Picks at his teeth, his rosewood instrument.
In brown nasality he shakes with song.

Which is my lady's throat and which her song?
And who will ask the singer which is true:
The beauty of the song or instrument?
The guitarist clears the thunder from his throat,
Briefly strangles, hawks against the wall.
Or was that beauty, and could that beauty move?

I would not sing though all your ladies move
The gods to weep with your blue, essential song.
I heard a thousand birds upon a wall
With nests of eggs so musical, so true,
That families could breakfast on the throat
Of song, with knife and fork for instrument.

But could I live, a silent instrument,
Blowing candles as my bellows move?
O my lady, last night I watched your throat,
Your breast, your reddened lips enclose a song.
Which do I love? I tell that song is true,
But flesh must turn alone to face the wall.

Your voice is like the waves that shake my wall.
Its waveforms play a passive instrument.
The seawracked sailor knows that both are true:
The racing wave, the waves that never move.

Wrenched between the instrument and song,
I cannot kiss the music of her throat.

Must I tear the music from her throat
Until her voice runs greenly through the wall,
The instrument lies battered by the song,
The song runs foaming from the instrument?
Then, my quiet lady, will you move,
Dissolve in earth, and leave your song as true;

Or place my throat beneath an instrument?
The blade will move; I'll roll against the wall.
My blood will sing, but will its song be true?

TO LOVE THAT CAME TO NOTHING

Tonight's black rain turns the night
Down low, below the glance of lamps
Swung in the corners of our sight.
We lie apart, as disarmed camps
For whom the shocking war is done;
Diplomacy must tell what's won.

You lie upon my arm, where sleep
Stitches at my thumbs, all thumbs;
Where clumsiness and lightness keep
The ancient dance that thrills and numbs.
But as we ached in our closest stance,
We knew no tune survived the dance.

HAPPILY BECAUSE APRIL

Happily because April wore
Your flashing pelt, I sing
This praise of everything:
Water, sycamore,
The breathing of the wine
Across your lips to mine.

Deeply as the grass
Was taught by comb in hair
To undulate in air,
Our passions sift and pass,
And in your eyes, the wind
And water whorl and blend.

But yellow takes the oak.
And autumn takes the heart.
Love and counterpart
Fall away in smoke.
I celebrate the stone,
The limits of the bone.

HOW SO LOVELY WALKS THE WIND

How so lovely walks the wind
Beside the chafing waterwheel.
But soon the sliding stream will rind
And winds will hollow at the mill.

Now that wind will have its way
I take my lovely girl in hand
Deep in shaken grass, and lay
Her back into the shape of wind.

How so deeply will we lie
When all the greenery burns low
That wind will roll its caissons by
A mound of summer in the snow.

THE ELEMENTS

How bitterly I fell from sense
To take my breathing through her hair.
She bedded with the elements:
Water, fire, earth and air.

We drowned the world of innocence.
From our husks no son or daughter
Rises from the elements:
Fire, air, earth and water.

I saw us through a shrinking lens;
Down we crumpled into birth
And scattered to the elements:
Air, water, fire and earth.

Let love be that intelligence
That rises from the funeral pyre
To sing a song of elements:
Earth, water, air and fire.

INDIANA UNIVERSITY POETRY SERIES

(all volumes hardbound unless otherwise indicated)